E♭ **Baritone Saxophone/Solo Clarinet**

ORIGINAL BIG BAND SOUNDS

Transcribed and Recreated by Jeff Hest
from the original recordings with original instrumentation

Project Editor: Larry Clark
Book Design: Ken Rehm

LITTLE BROWN JUG

By
BILL FINEGAN
Arranged by JEFF HEST

Eb Baritone Sax

4

DON'T GET AROUND MUCH ANYMORE

Music by
DUKE ELLINGTON
Arranged by JEFF HEST

E♭ Baritone Sax

PENNSYLVANIA 6-5000

Lyric by
CARL SIGMAN

Music by
JERRY GRAY
Arranged by JEFF HEST

E♭ Baritone Sax

STOMPIN' AT THE SAVOY

Lyric by
ANDY RAZAF

Music by
BENNY GOODMAN, CHICK WEBB and EDGAR SAMPSON
Arranged by JEFF HEST

Solo Clarinet

DON'T BE THAT WAY

Words by MITCHELL PARISH

Music by BENNY GOODMAN and
EDGAR SAMPSON
Arranged by JEFF HEST

Solo Clarinet

SONG OF INDIA

Solo Clarinet

By TOMMY DORSEY and RED BONE
Arranged by JEFF HEST

12

Solo Clarinet

𝆑 GRADUAL CRESC.

MOONLIGHT SERENADE

Lyric by
MITCHELL PARISH

Music by
GLENN MILLER
Arranged by JEFF HEST

Clarinet

SING, SING, SING
(Part I)

Words and Music by
LOUIS PRIMA
Arranged by JEFF HEST

Clarinet

SING, SING, SING
(Part II)

Words and Music by
LOUIS PRIMA
Arranged by JEFF HEST

Clarinet

Clarinet